PIGLING

A CINDERELLA STORY

A KOREAN TALE

GRAPHIC UNIVERSE™

STORY BY
DAN JOLLEY

PENCILS AND INKS BY
ANNE TIMMONS

CHINA

NORTH
KOREA

YELLOW

SEA

SOUTH
KOREA

PIGLING

A CINDERELLA STORY

A KOREAN TALE

EAST

SEA

JAPAN

PACIFIC

OCEAN

PIGLING IS A KOREAN CINDERELLA STORY. IT HAS BEEN TOLD THROUGHOUT KOREA FOR CENTURIES. MANY DIFFERENT VERSIONS OF THE STORY EXIST, BUT THEY ALL TELL OF A YOUNG GIRL WHO SUFFERS AT THE HANDS OF A WICKED STEPMOTHER. THE STORIES ALSO FEATURE A HELPFUL GOBLIN THAT REVEALS ITSELF IN THE FORM OF FRIENDLY FOREST CREATURES. THESE CREATURES STEP FORWARD TO ASSIST THE HEROINE WHENEVER SHE NEEDS A HELPING HAND.

IN CREATING THIS ADAPTATION OF PIGLING, AUTHOR DAN JOLLEY RELIED ON SEVERAL TELLINGS OF THE TALE, INCLUDING WILLIAM ELLIOT GRIFFIS'S PIGLING AND HER PROUD SISTER AS IT APPEARS IN OLIVE BEAUPRÉ MILLER'S THROUGH FAIRY HALLS. JOLLEY ALSO WORKED WITH CONSULTANT MINSOOK KIM, PH.D., OF THE UNIVERSITY OF CALIFORNIA, BERKELEY, TO ENSURE THAT THE STORY'S DETAILS ARE HISTORICALLY ACCURATE. ARTIST ANNE TIMMONS REFERRED TO NUMEROUS HISTORICAL SOURCES AND WORKED CLOSELY WITH KIM TO BRING THE STORY'S DYNAMIC IMAGERY TO LIFE.

STORY BY DAN JOLLEY

PENCILS AND INKS BY ANNE TIMMONS

COLORING BY HI-FI DESIGN

LETTERING BY MARSHALL DILLON AND TERRI DELGADO

CONSULTANT: MINSOOK KIM, PH.D., UNIVERSITY OF CALIFORNIA, BERKELEY

Graphic Universe™
A division of Lerner Publishing Group, Inc.
241 First Avenue North
Minneapolis, MN 55401 U.S.A.

Website address: www.lernerbooks.com

Library of Congress Cataloging-in-Publication Data

Jolley, Dan.
    Pigling : a Cinderella story : a Korean tale / story by Dan Jolley ; pencils and inks by Anne Timmons.
      p. cm. — (Graphic myths and legends)
    Includes index.
      ISBN 978-0-8225-7174-2 (lib. bdg. : alk. paper)
      1. Graphic novels. I. Timmons, Anne. II. Title. III. Title: Cinderella story: a Korean tale.
    PN6727.J58P55 2008
    741.5'973—dc22   2007040891

Manufactured in the United States of America
1 2 3 4 5 6 - DP - 14 13 12 11 10 09

TABLE OF CONTENTS

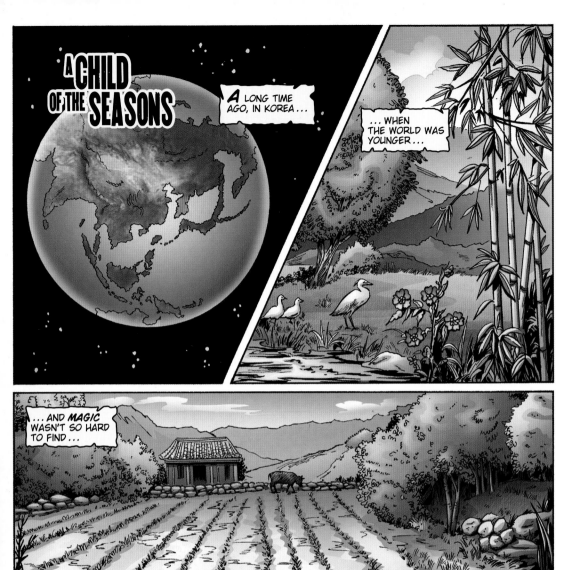

A CHILD OF THE SEASONS

A LONG TIME AGO, IN KOREA ...

... WHEN THE WORLD WAS YOUNGER ...

... AND *MAGIC* WASN'T SO HARD TO FIND ...

... AN OLD MAN LIVED WITH HIS BEAUTIFUL WIFE ON A FARM.

THEY WERE *HAPPY* TOGETHER, BUT MORE THAN ANYTHING ELSE IN THE WORLD, THEY WANTED A *BABY*.

FOR YEARS AND YEARS, THEY WAITED ...

... UNTIL *FINALLY* THE WOMAN LEARNED THAT SHE WAS *WITH CHILD.*

THE WOMAN GAVE BIRTH TO A *DAUGHTER.* SHE AND HER HUSBAND WERE *THRILLED...*

... AND THE OLD MAN IMMEDIATELY PLANTED A *PEAR TREE* IN CELEBRATION.

AS THE OLD MAN STOOD ADMIRING THE TREE, HE THOUGHT OF THE PERFECT NAME FOR THE BABY.

PEAR BLOSSOM! THAT'S WHAT WE SHALL CALL OUR DAUGHTER!

7

PEAR BLOSSOM'S PARENTS LOVED HER WITH ALL THEIR HEARTS. THEY WORKED HARD TO GIVE THEIR DAUGHTER THE BEST OF EVERYTHING.

IN THE SPRING, HER MOTHER WOVE A PINK RIBBON IN HER DAUGHTER'S HAIR. THE RIBBON WAS AS LUMINOUS AS THE BLOOMS ON THE PEAR TREE.

IN THE HEAT OF SUMMER, SHE USED A RIBBON OF GOLD.

AND IN THE AUTUMN, SHE MADE PEAR BLOSSOM A BRILLIANT YELLOW GOWN TO MATCH THE CHANGING LEAVES.

PEAR BLOSSOM'S FATHER DIDN'T KNOW WHAT TO DO AFTER THE LOSS OF HIS WIFE. "WHO WILL CARE FOR MY DAUGHTER?" HE CRIED.

AND SO, EVEN THOUGH HIS HEART WAS STILL BROKEN ...

... HE TOOK PEAR BLOSSOM TO THE VILLAGE AND WENT TO SEE A MATCHMAKER. HE KNEW SHE COULD FIND HIM WHAT HE BELIEVED HE NEEDED: A NEW WIFE.

OH, I THINK I HAVE *JUST* THE ANSWER TO YOUR PROBLEM!

WE'LL DO THREE IN ONE! A WIFE FOR YOU AND A MOTHER AND SISTER FOR YOUR YOUNG ONE.

AND SO PEAR BLOSSOM AND HER FATHER MET THE *WIDOW* THE MATCHMAKER HAD SPOKEN OF, AS WELL AS HER *DAUGHTER*... A GIRL PEAR BLOSSOM'S AGE, NAMED VIOLET.

PEAR BLOSSOM'S FATHER VERY QUICKLY *MARRIED* THE WIDOW...

...WHO IMMEDIATELY TOLD PEAR BLOSSOM TO CALL HER *OMONI*, WHICH MEANS "MOTHER."

OMONI AND VIOLET MOVED INTO PEAR BLOSSOM'S HOME THE NEXT DAY.

13

A NEW FAMILY

PEAR BLOSSOM TRIED HARD TO MAKE OMONI AND VIOLET FEEL WELCOME IN THEIR NEW SURROUNDINGS.

BUT THAT MORNING, AT BREAKFAST... IS WHEN ALL THE TROUBLE STARTED.

PEAR BLOSSOM, THIS IS *COLD.* STOKE THE FIRE, AND WARM IT UP FOR US.

OH—I'M VERY SORRY, OMONI. I'LL HEAT IT UP AT ONCE.

A FEW MINUTES LATER...

HERE, OMONI— THIS SHOULD BE MORE TO YOUR LIKING.

OW! OW! IT'S TOO HOT, I BURNED MY TONGUE!

SEE WHAT YOU'VE DONE? YOU'VE HURT YOUR SISTER! HOW DARE YOU!

I'M SORRY. I'M SO SORRY. I DIDN'T MEAN TO—

YOU'VE DONE MORE THAN ENOUGH, LITTLE GIRL. GET OUT OF OUR SIGHT!

BUT THERE WAS ONE VERY IMPORTANT THING THAT PEAR BLOSSOM DIDN'T REALIZE.

EVEN AS TIRED AND DIRTY AND MISERABLE AS SHE WAS ... SHE WAS *BEAUTIFUL*.

PEAR BLOSSOM WAS THE MOST BEAUTIFUL GIRL FOR THOUSANDS OF MILES AROUND ...

... AND OMONI AND VIOLET *KNEW IT.*

THEIR HEARTS WERE *EATEN* UP WITH *JEALOUSY* OF PEAR BLOSSOM.

14

A SAD FUTURE

*F*INALLY, AFTER THREE LONG, PAINFUL MONTHS OF INSULTS AND ABUSE, PEAR BLOSSOM COULDN'T TAKE IT ANYMORE . . .

. . . AND DECIDED TO APPROACH HER *FATHER*. HE WAS THE MAN OF THE HOUSE. SURELY, HE COULD DO SOMETHING TO HELP HER.

SHE WASN'T SURE OF WHAT TO SAY OR HOW TO SAY IT, THOUGH. HER FATHER HAD GROWN SO MUCH *WEAKER* SINCE HER MOTHER DIED.

BUT HE LOVES ME, PEAR BLOSSOM THOUGHT. *HE'LL UNDERSTAND. HE'LL MAKE THEM STOP TORTURING ME.*

FATHER ...?

EH? *OH!* MY LOVELY DAUGHTER, HOW ARE YOU? DOING WELL, I TRUST?

WELL, FATHER, THAT'S WHAT I CAME TO TALK TO YOU ABOUT. I—

GOOD, GOOD. GLAD TO HEAR IT.

BUT—

BUT I—

YOU RUN ALONG NOW. YOUR FATHER'S VERY TIRED.

NOW, NOW. IT'S NOT POLITE TO INTERRUPT ME WHEN I'M TRYING TO NAP. YOU WERE TAUGHT BETTER.

RUN ALONG, AND DON'T FORGET TO MIND YOUR NEW MOTHER. SHE KNOWS WHAT'S *BEST* FOR YOU, AFTER ALL.

PEAR BLOSSOM'S HEART *BROKE AGAIN* WHEN SHE REALIZED HER FATHER WOULD BE *NO HELP AT ALL.*

SHE WAS IN THIS SITUATION *ON HER OWN.*

SO PEAR BLOSSOM RESIGNED HERSELF TO HER NEW LIFE OF LONELINESS AND MISERY...

...AND YEARS WENT BY. GRADUALLY PEAR BLOSSOM FORGOT WHAT IT WAS LIKE TO BE HAPPY.

OMONI AND VIOLET NEVER LET UP ON THEIR TAUNTS AND INSULTS AND ABUSE.

BECAUSE THE OLDER PEAR BLOSSOM GOT...

17

...THE MORE *BEAUTIFUL* SHE BECAME.

AND THEY *HATED* HER FOR IT.

EVEN THOUGH OMONI SHOWED HER OWN DAUGHTER EVERY KIND OF MOTHERLY AFFECTION AND DEVOTION...

...SHE LAY AWAKE EVERY NIGHT TRYING TO COME UP WITH NEW WAYS TO MAKE PEAR BLOSSOM MISERABLE.

AN UNEXPECTED FRIEND

BUT THEN, ONE DAY, SHORTLY AFTER PEAR BLOSSOM TURNED *EIGHTEEN*, HER LUCK BEGAN TO CHANGE...

EVEN AS OMONI'S SPITEFULNESS TOWARD PEAR BLOSSOM GREW.

WE'RE GOING OUT FOR A WHILE, PIGLING. BY THE TIME WE COME BACK, I WANT THAT JAR *FILLED* WITH *WATER*.

I, AH, I'M *SORRY*, OMONI, BUT I DON'T UNDERSTAND. THERE'S A *HOLE* IN THE JAR—

I DON'T WANT TO HEAR *EXCUSES*, PIGLING! GET THAT JAR FILLED, OR I'LL MAKE YOU WISH YOU HAD!

WHAT AM I GOING TO DO?

IS THERE NO ONE IN THIS WORLD WHO CAN HELP ME?

JUG-FULL, JUG-FULL

... WHAT?

JUG-FULL

DON'T WORRY

JUG-FULL

AH!

WERE YOU—? WAS THAT—?

WERE YOU *TALKING*?

DON'T WORRY

JUG-FULL

PEAR BLOSSOM REALIZED—AS STRANGE AS IT SEEMED—THAT THIS *TALKING FROG* WAS GOING TO *HELP* HER.

HOLE-PLUGGED JUG-FULL

OH! HOW *DELIGHTFUL*! THANK YOU FOR YOUR *HELP*, MASTER FROG!

I'M FRIENDS WITH A MAGIC FROG ... HMMM HMM HMM HMMMM ...

THE INCIDENT WITH THE WATER JAR JUST MADE OMONI ALL THE MORE EAGER TO RUIN PEAR BLOSSOM'S LIFE. THE NEXT DAY ...

PIGLING! COME HERE!

YES, OMONI?

VIOLET AND I ARE GOING OUT. BY THE TIME WE GET BACK, I WANT ALL THIS RICE HULLED.

BY HAND.

BY HAND? BUT, OMONI, I DON'T THINK I CAN DO ALL THAT BEFORE YOU—

I'M SICK OF YOUR EXCUSES, PIGLING! GET IT DONE, OR YOU'LL BE SORRY!

TEE-HEE-HEE

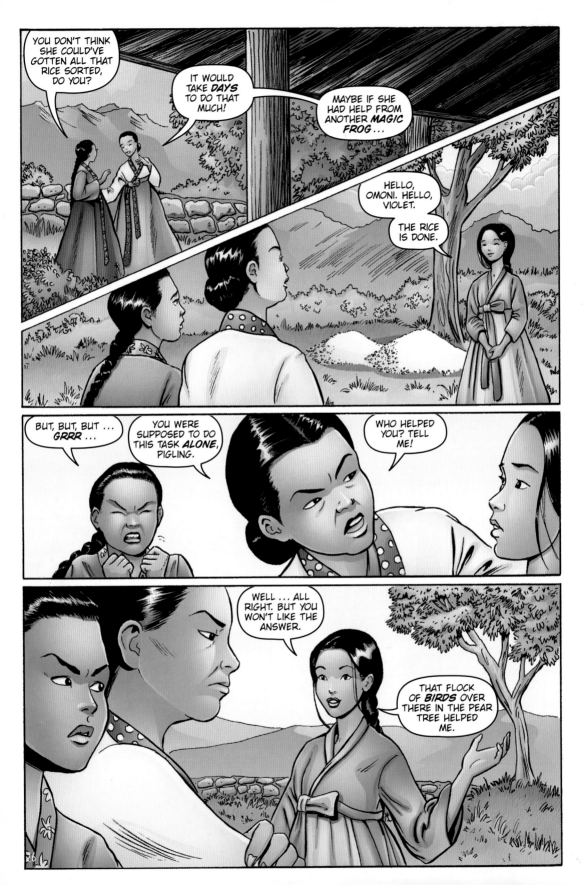

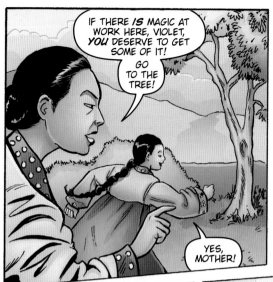

IF THERE *IS* MAGIC AT WORK HERE, VIOLET, *YOU* DESERVE TO GET SOME OF IT!

GO TO THE TREE!

YES, MOTHER!

GIVE ME YOUR MAGIC, BIRDS!

I'M MORE WORTHY OF IT THAN THAT STUPID *PIGLING!*

CHEAT! CHEAT!

CHEAT! CHEAT!

EEEEEEE!

MOTHER! THE BIRDS HURT ME, AND IT'S ALL *PIGLING'S* FAULT!

JUST YOU WAIT, LITTLE PIG! YOU'LL PAY *DEARLY* FOR THIS!

A FESTIVAL APPROACHES

Days went by as Omoni planned and plotted, trying to figure out the best way to torment Pear Blossom.

Soon the village began to prepare for a **FESTIVAL**.

Pear Blossom found herself sewing a **DRESS** for **VIOLET** . . .

. . . and preparing huge baskets filled with delicious food for her stepmother and stepsister.

It was then that Omoni finally decided what to do.

Thank you, pigling. You have done your work well.

AND AS SUCH, YOU MAY ATTEND THE FESTIVAL ALSO.

REALLY? DO YOU... DO YOU *MEAN* IT?

OF COURSE.

AS SOON AS YOU'VE *WEEDED ALL THE RICE PADDIES.*

AND HERE'S A BASKET OF *TURNIP TOPS* TO KEEP YOUR *STRENGTH* UP WHILE YOU'RE WORKING.

THAT'S A FIT MEAL FOR A LITTLE *PIGLING* LIKE YOURSELF.

A WHIRLWIND ROMANCE

IS THERE **NO ONE** IN THIS WORLD WHO CAN **HELP** ME?

THEN SUDDENLY A **FIERCE WIND** BEGAN TO BLOW, AND A SMALL **TORNADO** CAME RUSHING TOWARD THE RICE PADDIES.

PEAR BLOSSOM DIDN'T KNOW WHAT TO THINK. SHE KNEW SHE COULDN'T OUTRUN SUCH A THING. BUT THEN SOMETHING HAPPENED...

... THAT LEFT HER COMPLETELY SPEECHLESS.

PEAR BLOSSOM HAD NEVER SEEN A *NOBLEMAN* SUCH AS THIS BEFORE. BADLY STARTLED AND FRIGHTENED, SHE DID THE ONLY THING SHE COULD THINK OF TO DO.

34

A MOMENT'S PEACE

*B*Y THE TIME SHE REACHED THE FESTIVAL, PEAR BLOSSOM'S HEART HAD STOPPED BEATING SO FAST AND SHE DIDN'T EVEN MISS HER SANDAL THAT MUCH.

AND SO, FOR THE FIRST TIME IN A VERY, VERY LONG TIME . . .

. . . PEAR BLOSSOM GOT TO ENJOY HERSELF A LITTLE BIT.

A VERY LITTLE BIT, AS IT TURNED OUT.

PIGLING!

35

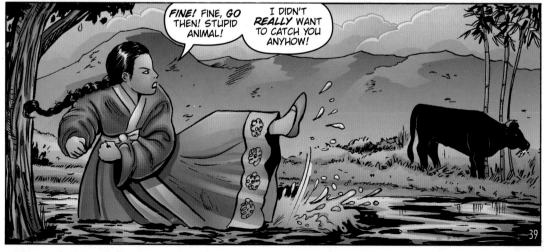

A NEW LIFE

GRUMBLE GRUMBLE GRUMBLE

DAUGHTER? WHAT *HAPPENED* TO YOU? YOU LOOK...

TERRIBLE.

DID YOU CATCH THE MAGIC OX OR—

ATTENTION! I DEMAND THE ATTENTION OF EVERYONE HERE, ON BEHALF OF THE *MAGISTRATE SU-WEN!*

THE MAGISTRATE SEEKS TO FIND A *YOUNG WOMAN* HE BELIEVES TO BE IN ATTENDANCE HERE...

...A YOUNG WOMAN WHO MAY BE WEARING ONLY *ONE SANDAL.*

HA! THEY'VE COME TO *ARREST* YOU FOR THAT *FRUIT* YOU STOLE, YOU PIGGY LITTLE *THIEF!*

IT'S HER! IT'S HER! SHE'S THE ONE YOU'RE LOOKING FOR—SHE'S GOT ONLY ONE SANDAL!

NOW, PIGLING! *NOW* YOU'LL GET WHAT YOU DESERVE!

NO! *WAIT!* I'M *SERIOUS! TWO SANDALS!*

ONE ON EACH *FOOT!*

I KNEW I WANTED YOU TO BE MY WIFE FROM THE SECOND I SAW YOU ON THE ROAD.

IT WOULD BE... A *GREAT HONOR*... IF YOU WERE TO ACCEPT ME AS YOUR HUSBAND.

WHEN PEAR BLOSSOM LOOKED INTO THE MAGISTRATE'S EYES, SHE SAW HOW *KIND* AND *STRONG* AND *GOOD* HE WAS.

AND SHE KNEW THAT IT WAS HER *DESTINY* TO SAY *YES*.

THE MAGISTRATE SENT GO-BETWEENS TO PEAR BLOSSOM'S FATHER...

...AND ARRANGED FOR A GRAND WEDDING THE FOLLOWING SPRING.

EVERYONE WHO CAME TO IT AGREED...

PEAR BLOSSOM MOVED AWAY FROM HER FATHER AND OMONI AND VIOLET, AND INTO THE MAGISTRATE'S HOUSE...

...WHERE HIS PARENTS... HER *NEW* PARENTS... GREETED HER WITH LOVING, OPEN ARMS.

THAT WAS WHEN SHE *SAW* SOMETHING IN THE GRAND HOUSE'S *COURTYARD*... SOMETHING THAT TOOK HER BREATH AWAY.

AND AS SHE *LAUGHED* AND *DANCED* AND *SPUN* AMID THE TWELVE *BEAUTIFUL PEAR TREES* THAT GREW THERE...

PEAR BLOSSOM KNEW SHE HAD FOUND HER *HOME*.

GLOSSARY AND PRONUNCIATION GUIDE

GO—BETWEEN: a person who helps people to communicate or to reach an agreement. Pear Blossom's future husband sent go-betweens to Pear Blossom's father to reach an agreement about the couple's marriage.

HULL: to separate the outer covering from a seed

MAGISTRATE (*maj*-uh-strate): an official who rules over a land or a nation

MATCHMAKER: a person who brings unmarried people together to arrange a marriage

NOBLEMAN: a man who is born to an important family or who holds an important position

OMONI (aw-*maw*-nee): the Korean word for "mother"

OX: a large mammal related to the cow

PADDY: wet land where rice grows

PROPOSAL: a suggestion or an offer. *Proposal* often refers to a marriage offer.

TORNADO: a strong windstorm accompanied by a funnel-shaped cloud

WIDOW: a woman whose husband has died

original pencil sketch from page 26

FURTHER READING AND WEBSITES

Climo, Shirley. *The Korean Cinderella*. New York: HarperCollins Publishers, 1993. Climo's picture-book version of the Korean Cinderella story features detailed paintings and Korean words and expressions.

Fleischman, Paul. *Glass Slipper, Gold Sandal: A Worldwide Cinderella*. New York: Henry Holt, 2007. This enchanting title marries many different traditions. It interweaves seventeen Cinderella stories into one multicultural fairy tale.

Holman, Sheri. *Sondok: Princess of the Moon and Stars*. New York: Scholastic, 2002. Read the fictional diary of Princess Sondok, the girl who became queen of Silla, South Korea, in A.D. 632.

Hidden Korea: Culture
http://www.pbs.org/hiddenkorea/
Learn interesting facts about Korean culture at this website from PBS.

Time for Kids: South Korea
http://www.timeforkids.com/TFK/hh/goplaces/main/0,20344,927166,00.html
Explore South Korea at this site, which includes a sightseeing guide, a fun quiz, and e-cards you can send to your friends.

CREATING *PIGLING: A CINDERELLA STORY*

To create *Pigling: A Cinderella Story*, author Dan Jolley relied on various versions of the story, including William Elliot Griffis's *Pigling and Her Proud Sister* as it appears in Olive Beaupré Miller's *Through Fairy Halls*. Jolley shaped his adaptation of the tale in consultation with Minsook Kim, Ph.D., of the University of California, Berkeley. Artist Anne Timmons consulted various historical sources while completing artwork for the book. She worked closely with Kim to ensure accuracy in her depictions of Korean customs and culture.

INDEX

ABOUT THE AUTHOR AND THE ARTIST

DAN JOLLEY began his writing career in the early nineties. His limited series *Obergeist* was voted Best Horror Comic of 2001 by *Wizard Magazine*, and his DC Comics project *JSA: The Unholy Three* received an Eisner Award nomination (the comics industry's highest honor) for Best Limited Series of 2003. In recent years, he has cowritten two novels based on licensed properties: *Star Trek SCE: Some Assembly Required* and *Vengeance*, from the television series *Angel*. May 2007 saw the debut of Jolley's first solo novel series, an original young adult sci-fi espionage story called *Alex Unlimited*, published by a joint venture of TokyoPop and HarperCollins. Jolley lives in Cary, North Carolina, where he works as a computer game designer for Icarus Studios.

ANNE TIMMONS was born in Portland, Oregon, and received her Bachelor of Fine Arts degree from Oregon State University. In addition to her collaboration with Trina Robbins on the Lulu Award-winning *GoGirl!*, Timmons's work includes the Eisner-nominated *Dignifying Science* and the comic-book version of *Star Trek: Deep Space Nine*. She has illustrated and painted covers for children's books and provided interior and cover art for regional and national magazines, including *Wired*, *Portland Review*, and *Comic Book Artist*. Timmons's art also appears in the anthology *9-11: Artists Respond* and is now part of the Prints and Photographs collection at the Library of Congress. Timmons and Robbins recently collaborated on a graphic novel adaptation of Jane Austen's *Northanger Abbey*, which came out in 2007. Samples of Timmons's art can be seen at http://www.annetimmons.com.